KU-627-665

9112000401297

dabble lab

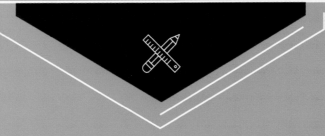

MOTION
PROJECTS TO BUILD ON

BY MARNE VENTURA

raintree

a Capstone company — publishers for children

Raintree is an imprint of Capstone Global Library Limited, a company incorporated in England and Wales having its registered office at 264 Banbury Road, Oxford, OX2 7DY – Registered company number: 6695582

www.raintree.co.uk
myorders@raintree.co.uk

Text © Capstone Global Library Limited 2019
The moral rights of the proprietor have been asserted.

All rights reserved. No part of this publication may be reproduced in any form or by any means (including photocopying or storing it in any medium by electronic means and whether or not transiently or incidentally to some other use of this publication) without the written permission of the copyright owner, except in accordance with the provisions of the Copyright, Designs and Patents Act 1988 or under the terms of a licence issued by the Copyright Licensing Agency, Barnard's Inn, 86 Fetter Lane, London, EC4A 1EN (www.cla.co.uk). Applications for the copyright owner's written permission should be addressed to the publisher.

Edited by Mari Bolte
Designed by Heidi Thompson
Original illustrations © Capstone Global Library Limited 2019
Picture research by Morgan Walters
Production by Laura Manthe
Originated by Capstone Global Library Ltd
Printed and bound in India

ISBN 978 1 4747 7541 0
22 21 20 19 18
10 9 8 7 6 5 4 3 2 1

British Library Cataloguing in Publication Data
A full catalogue record for this book is available from the British Library.

Acknowledgements
We would like to thank the following for permission to reproduce photographs: all images by Capstone Studio, Karon Dubke; Shutterstock: 4 Girls 1 Boy, (grid) design element throughout, Alexyz3d, 5, VectorPot (gears) design element throughout.

Every effort has been made to contact copyright holders of material reproduced in this book. Any omissions will be rectified in subsequent printings if notice is given to the publisher.

All the internet addresses (URLs) given in this book were valid at the time of going to press. However, due to the dynamic nature of the internet, some addresses may have changed, or sites may have changed or ceased to exist since publication. While the author and publisher regret any inconvenience this may cause readers, no responsibility for any such changes can be accepted by either the author or the publisher.

BRENT LIBRARIES	
KIN	
91120000401297	
Askews & Holts	26-Apr-2019
J531.11 JUNIOR NON-F	£13.99

CONTENTS

REV IT UP!

How high, far or fast can you go? The challenge of how to get from one place to another is one that we'll never stop trying to solve. The sky's the limit – literally! – as we fly, float, scoot, pedal and drive our way towards the next amazing vehicle.

Learn the science behind history's greatest locomotion discoveries by testing them out yourself. You may be starting out with simple wheels and axles, but you could be speeding down the track faster than you think.

MOVE ALONG

Locomotion is the ability to move from one place to another. Explore the most basic way to get ahead – gravity! Build yourself a downhill racer and test it out on a track that's made for speed.

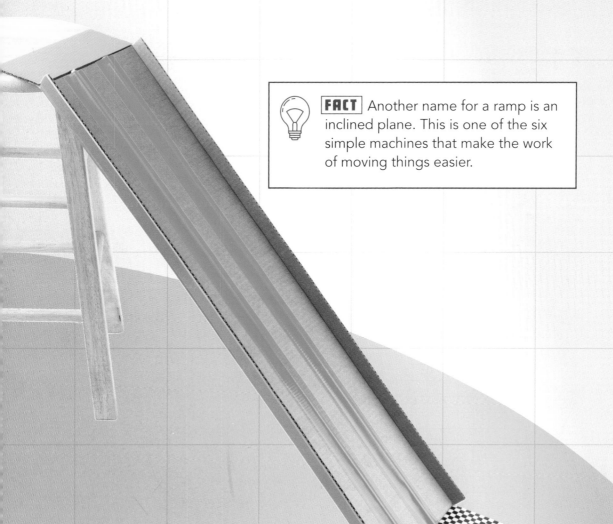

> **FACT** Another name for a ramp is an inclined plane. This is one of the six simple machines that make the work of moving things easier.

TEST TRACK

To test most of your cars, you'll need a track! Build a tilted track and let gravity do all the work.

YOU'LL NEED

> utility knife

> large cardboard box

> metre stick

> strong tape

> two 90-cm- (36-inch-) long
  6 mm (¼ inch) dowels

STEPS

1 Ask an adult to use the utility knife to cut a 20-by-90-centimetre (9-by-36-inch) strip of cardboard.

2 Use the metre stick to draw two lines on the cardboard to make three tracks.

3 Tape the dowels over the lines you've drawn.

4 Ask an adult to cut two 2.5-by-90-cm (1-by-36-inch) lengths of cardboard.

5 Tape them to the sides of the track.

6 Ask an adult to cut two 10-by-23-cm (4-by-9-inch) rectangles of cardboard.

7 Tape them to the ends of the track.

8 Lean the ramp against a table or chair.

FACT When you place your car at the top of the ramp (inclined plane), two forces make it speed downwards. One is the force of gravity. This is the force made by Earth's mass that holds us on the planet. The other is the force of the ramp that prevents the car from falling through it. For another experiment, try changing how steep your ramp is.

7

CLOTHES PEG RACERS

Can you imagine a world without cars, bikes, lorries and buses? Wheels make the work of moving things and people so much easier. Find a few materials around the house and turn them into this cool racing car. Decorate your car in bright colours and make it go!

YOU'LL NEED

> three wooden clothes pegs

> paint and paintbrushes

> scissors

> three drinking straws

> hot glue and hot glue gun

> 12 small plastic wheels

> six cotton buds

> three small paper cups

> Test Track

> tape

> small weights

STEPS

1 Decorate the clothes pegs with paint. Let the paint dry.

2 Cut two 2.5-cm (1-inch) pieces of straw.

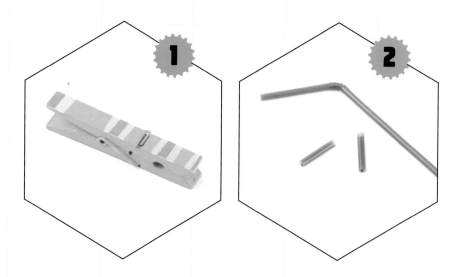

3 Cut off the ends of the cotton buds.

4 Put a dab of glue into the centre of one wheel. Insert one end of the cotton bud stick.

5 Thread one straw onto the cotton bud stick.

6 Glue on the second wheel. You now have a wheel and axle.

7 Repeat steps 4–6 for a second wheel and axle.

8 Clip one axle in the front of one of the clothes pegs. Glue the other axle inside the clothes peg near the spring.

9 Repeat steps 2–8 to make two more cars.

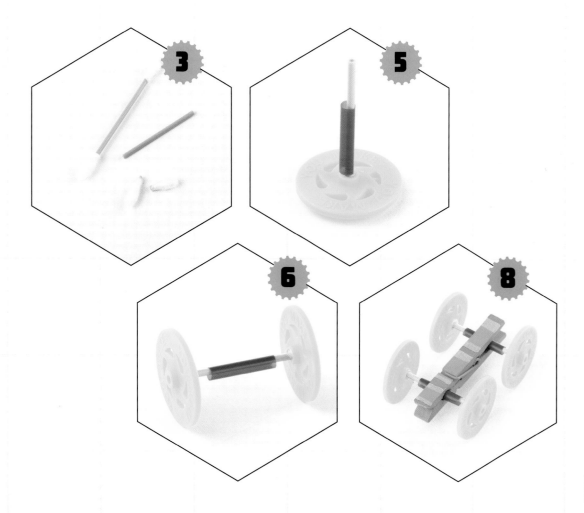

10 Place a line of cups upside down on the floor. They should be about 8 cm (3 inches) past the end of the ramp.

11 Race your clothes peg cars down the ramp. See how far they push the paper cups. Time them to see how fast they get to the base.

12 Now tape weights to the tops of your cars. Does the time change? Does it matter if you tape the weights to the front or back of the car? Try varying the amount of weight you add.

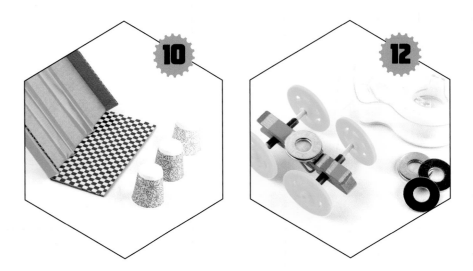

 FACT How do wheels help people work? Imagine dragging a box across the ground. The box and the ground rub together and create friction. This makes it hard to pull the box. Now imagine the box inside of a wagon. Only one spot on the wagon wheel touches the ground as it turns. This makes less friction, so it's easier to pull the wagon.

 FACT Historians have evidence that people in Mesopotamia used the first wheels to make pottery around 3500 BC. It took another 300 years for people to use wheels and axles to move chariots.

13 Change the angle of the Test Track. Make it flatter or steeper. Does the time change? Remove the weights, and time the car again. What are your results?

 FACT As the track's angle becomes steeper, the friction between the car and the track is decreased. But the weight that is added to the car increases the friction.

GETTING AHEAD

You've tested cars on a ramp. But can you make them move on flat ground? Test out wind-, elastic- and balloon-powered cars. Which car travels the fastest or furthest?

WIND POWER

Gravity is the easiest way to get something moving. But wind is another environmentally friendly resource! Although many wind-powered cars are assisted by batteries, fans or solar panels, you can make your own wind-powered vehicle with a simple sail.

 **YOU'LL NEED**

> plastic bin bag
> ruler
> marker pen
> scissors
> wooden skewers

> clear packing tape
> hot glue and hot glue gun
> wooden bead
> Clothes Peg Racer

STEPS

1   Flatten the bag on your work surface as best you can. Use the ruler and marker pen to measure and mark an 8-cm (3-inch) line along a corner of the bag.

2   Cut out the plastic triangle.

3   With an adult's help, cut one skewer to a length of 9 cm (3½ inches). Cut another skewer to 4 cm (1½ inches).

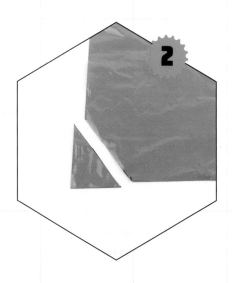

13

4 Open the triangle up so it's flat on your work surface. Place the long skewer over the fold at the centre of the triangle. Tape the skewer in place.

5 Repeat step 4 with the short skewer along a short edge of the triangle.

6 Fold the plastic triangle in half over the skewers. Tape the triangle shut.

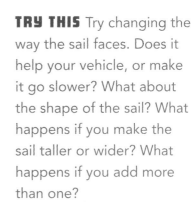

7 Glue the bead to the centre of a Clothes Peg Racer.

8 Glue the base of the sail to the bead.

9 Blow on your racer to make it move!

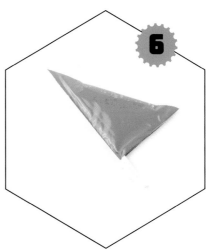

TRY THIS Try changing the way the sail faces. Does it help your vehicle, or make it go slower? What about the shape of the sail? What happens if you make the sail taller or wider? What happens if you add more than one?

Cars that speed down a track are fun. But what happens when you get a car on a flat, open space? This catapult car will shoot from point A to point B in a flash.

YOU'LL NEED

> scissors

> scrapbook paper

> toilet roll tube

> clear tape

> single hole punch

> two 9-cm- (3½-inch-) long wooden dowels

> hot glue and hot glue gun

> toy car wheels

> rubber band

> paperclip

> craft stick

STEPS

1 Cut a piece of scrapbook paper to fit around the tube. Tape in place.

2 Use the hole punch to make four holes in the tube for the axles.

3 Insert a dowel through each pair of holes. Trim as needed.

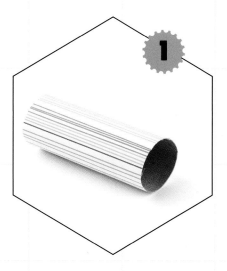

4 Glue the wheels to the ends of the skewers.

5 Thread the rubber band onto the paperclip.

6 Slip the other end of the paper clip onto one end of the tube. Hot glue in place.

7 Tape the other end of the rubber band to the end of the craft stick.

FACT A stretched-out rubber band stores elastic potential energy. When you release the car, the potential energy turns into kinetic energy and moves the car.

8 Put the car on the floor and hold in place. Pull the craft stick back as far as you can, and then release both the stick and the car.

9 Try it on your Test Track, but start it at the bottom. How far uphill can your Catapult Car go?

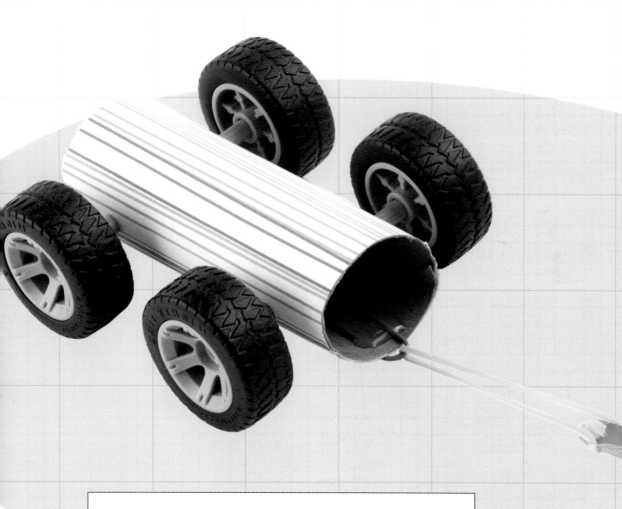

TRY THIS Try stacking a pyramid of small paper cups on the floor about 3 metres (10 feet) away from your launch point. Let the car crash into the cups. Test again, but place the cups further and further away each time.

PROJECT 2, LEVEL 3
BALLOON POWER

Rockets and jets use propulsion to move forwards. Make your own (safe) version with this balloon-powered car.

 **YOU'LL NEED**

> plastic water bottle
> strong tape
> skewers
> drinking straws
> hot glue and hot glue gun

> plastic wheels
> clear tape
> utility knife
> balloon

STEPS

1 Decorate the water bottle with tape.

2 Cut skewers and straws about 5 cm (2 inches) wider than the bottle.

3 Hot glue the end of one skewer to a wheel. Cover the skewer with a straw. Trim the straw if needed. Then glue on the other wheel. Repeat to make a second wheel and axle.

4 Tape the axles to the underside of the water bottle.

5 Ask an adult to cut a small x near the top of the water bottle. Push the straw through and out the neck of the bottle.

6 Tape a balloon to the end of the straw near the bottom of the bottle.

7 Blow into the straw to inflate the balloon. Then place your finger over the straw, put the car down on a flat surface and remove your finger.

 FACT Like the rubber bands in the Catapult Car, air stored in the balloon has potential energy. Covering the end of the straw with your finger keeps the compressed air inside. Once you let go, the potential energy is converted to kinetic energy. The movement of the air out of the balloon applies a force to the car that makes it move.

 FACT One of Newton's laws of motion is that for every action there is an equal and opposite reaction. When you inflate the balloon, it fills with air. When you open the straw, the air pushes out and moves the car. Real jet and rocket engines use gas explosions to push the crafts forward.

LIFT-OFF!

Staying on the road is a safe choice. Achieving lift-off is a step above! Take motion to the next level by exploring flight. Will you float to the ground safely or wipeout in a crash landing?

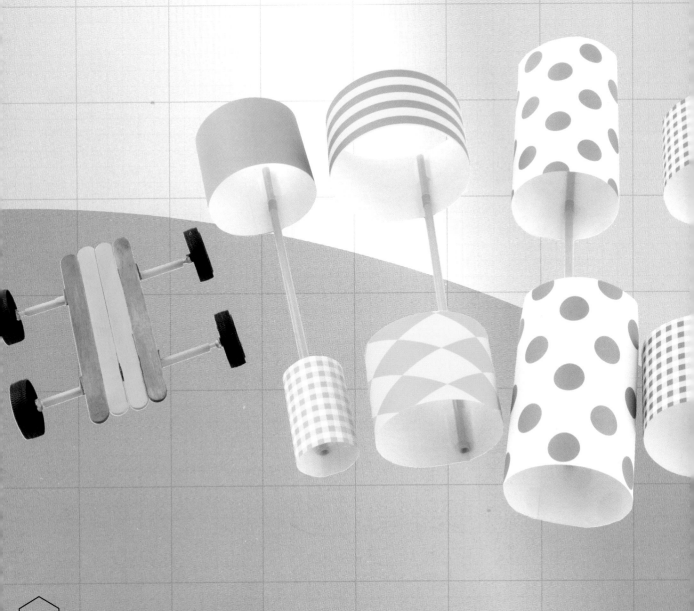

SUPER GLIDER CAR

The faster the glider is going when it takes off, the more lift the wings produce. Make your own aerodynamic O-wing glider cars, and see how far you can get them to fly.

YOU'LL NEED

> four 5-by-20-cm (2-by-8-inch) pieces of cardstock

> clear tape

> drinking straws

> five craft sticks

> hot glue and hot glue gun

> skewers

> plastic wheels

> two 10-by-20-cm (4-by-8-inch) pieces of cardstock

> one 5-by-25-cm (2-by-10-inch) piece of cardstock

> one 5-by-10-cm (2-by-4-inch) piece of cardstock

> Test Track

> electric fan

STEPS

1. Overlap the short ends of a 5-by-20-cm piece of cardstock to make a circle. Tape the ends together. Repeat with the second piece of cardstock.

2. Tape the circles to the ends of a drinking straw.

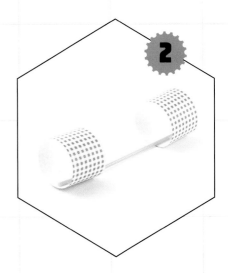

3 Lay four craft sticks side-by-side. Cut the fifth craft stick into two smaller rectangular pieces and place them the opposite way over the top of the four sticks. Glue in place.

4 Cut straws and skewers about 2.5 cm (1 inch) wider than the car.

5 Insert a skewer into a wheel. Slip the straw over the skewer. Then glue on the other wheel to make an axle.

6 Hot glue the straw axles to the car.

7 Tape the straw with the wings to the car.

8 Place the car on a table, 60 cm (2 feet) from the edge. Push it gently towards the edge.

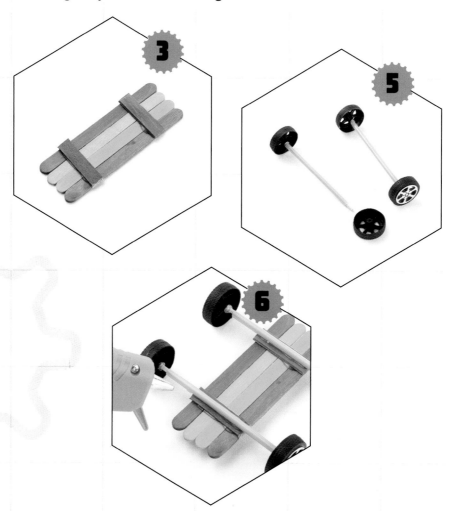

9 Repeat steps 1–8, but use the 10-by-20-cm pieces of cardstock to make the wings. Does the car glide better or worse?

10 Repeat steps 1–8, but use the 5-by-20-cm and 5-by-25-cm pieces of cardstock. Replace the wings you made in step 9 with your new wings. Position the smaller O-wing at the front of the car. Does the car glide better or worse?

11 Repeat steps 1–8, but use the 5-by-10-cm and 5-by-20-cm pieces of cardstock. Try out your new wings. Does the car glide better or worse?

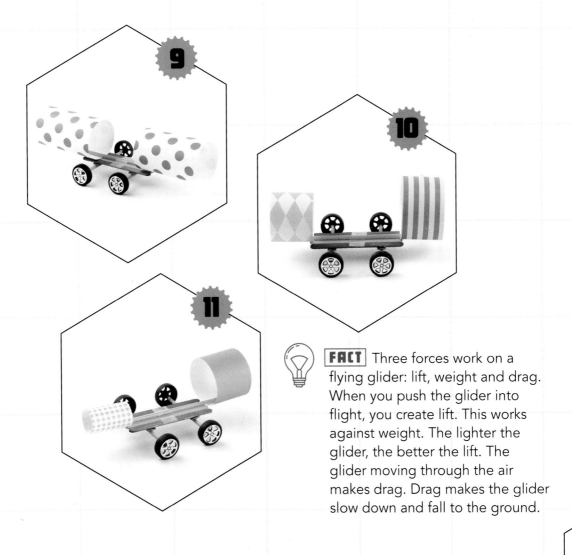

FACT Three forces work on a flying glider: lift, weight and drag. When you push the glider into flight, you create lift. This works against weight. The lighter the glider, the better the lift. The glider moving through the air makes drag. Drag makes the glider slow down and fall to the ground.

12 Place a fan at the edge of the table. Position it so it's pushing the air up. Test all your gliders. Does the fan help their flight?

13 Try using your Test Track. Line up the bottom edge of the track with the edge of the table. Does the extra speed affect how far your cars glide?

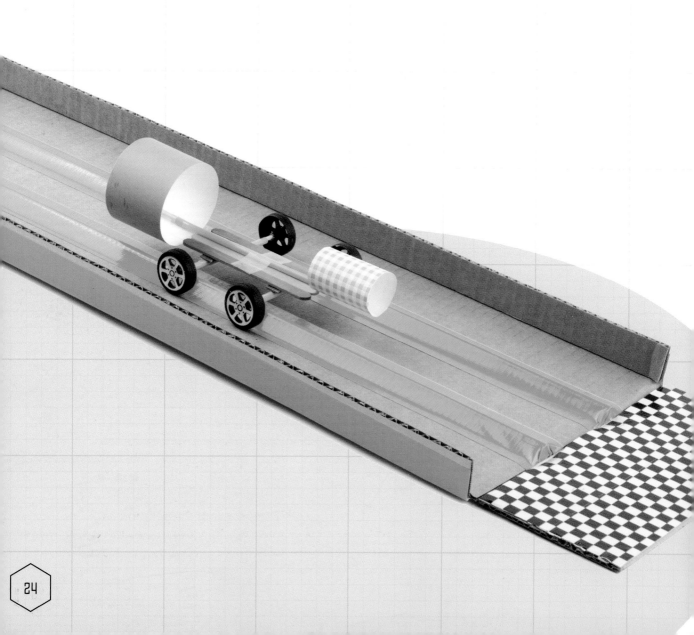

PARACHUTE LANDING

In a perfect world, everything would gently glide to a stop. But when you can't make the perfect landing, a parachute is what you need. Happy landing!

 **YOU'LL NEED**

> single hole punch
> small disposable cup
> scissors

> ruler
> plastic bin bag
> string

STEPS

1 Punch four holes evenly around the top of a cup.

2 Cut a 30-cm (12-inch) square from the bin bag.

3 Cut four 30-cm (12-inch) lengths of string.

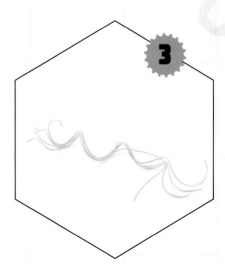

4 Scrunch a corner of the plastic square. Tie one end of a string around it. Repeat for each corner.

5 Tie the other end of each string to a hole in the cup.

6 Climb up to a high spot and drop the parachute. How long does it take to reach the ground?

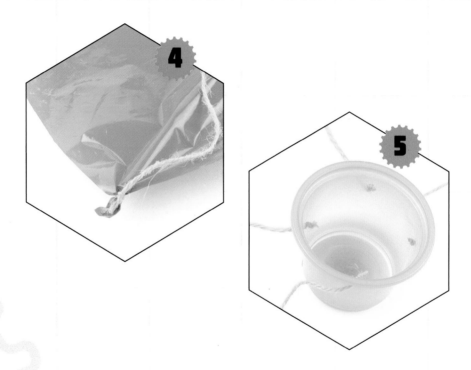

 FACT The force of gravity acts on your parachute when you let it drop from a height. Earth's gravity pulls it downwards quickly. So what does the parachute do? When air gets under a parachute, it creates resistance or drag. This slows the speed of the falling object, acting like a brake.

7 Repeat steps 1–4 to make a second parachute. Tie the strings to the same holes in your cup. Drop the cup again, and compare times.

8 Repeat steps 2–6, but cut a 40-cm (16-inch) square instead. Does the larger parachute speed up or slow down the landing?

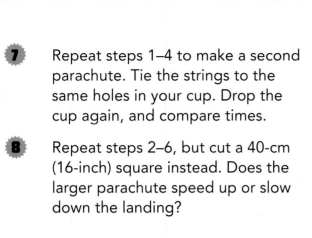

TRY THIS How confident are you in your parachuting skills? Add a passenger – such as an egg! – to the cup and find out.

To launch, hang-glider pilots run down a slope. Eventually they reach speeds fast enough to overcome gravity. Then their gliders take off! But how do they stay in the air? Find out how this glider defies gravity by folding your own.

YOU'LL NEED

> origami paper

> paperclip

> lightweight tape

> ruler

> scissors

> wooden skewers

STEPS

1   Valley fold edge to edge and unfold.

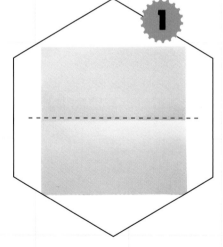

 FACT Like the Super Glider Car, hang-gliders must overcome drag, which is the force created when air strikes a moving object. Drag slows down moving objects. They also must overcome gravity. Lift is the force that helps aircraft rise from the ground and stay in the air. Air flows over the wings. As the hang-glider increases speed, the air pressure on top of the wing decreases. The higher air pressure underneath the wing results in lift.

2   Mark fold edge to edge and unfold.

3   Valley fold the edge to the mark fold made in step 2.

4   Valley fold the corners to the centre and unfold.

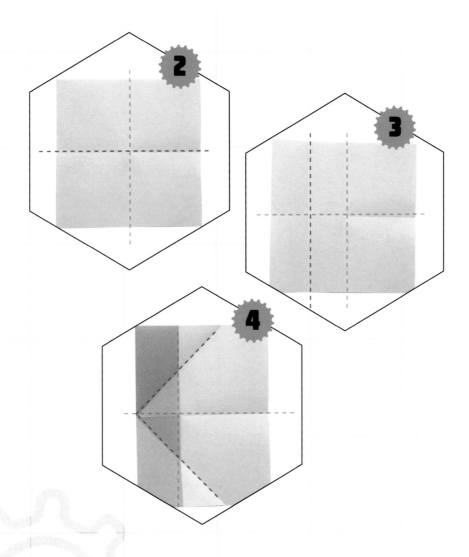

5 Reverse fold on the crease formed in step 4.

6 Valley fold the point.

7 Valley fold the flaps and tuck them into the pockets
   of the point.

8 Mountain fold the model in half and unfold.

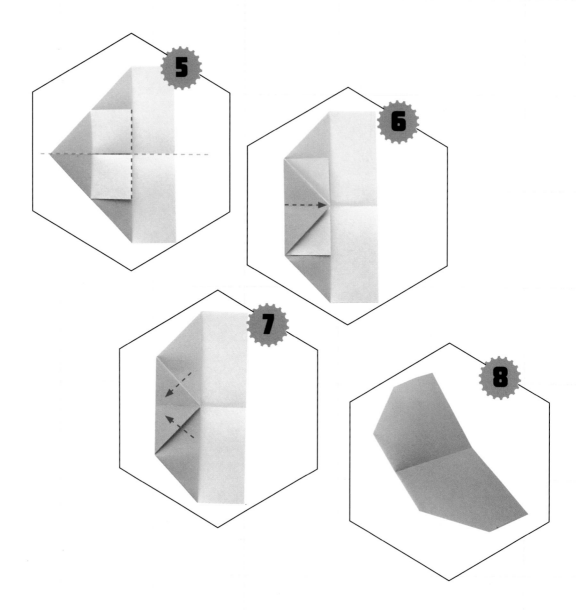

9 Repeat steps 1–8 until you have five hang-gliders. Set one glider, Hang-Glider 1, aside.

10 Slip a paperclip over the nose of Hang-Glider 2. Set aside.

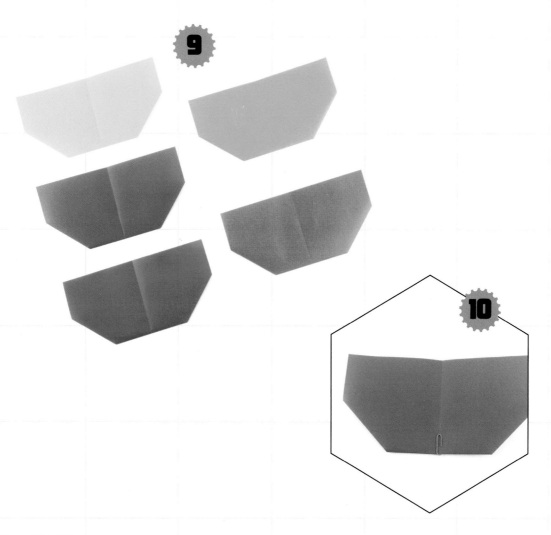

 FACT The first flexible wing hang-glider was created in the late 1940s. Its wings were used like a parachute. But it could also be steered, and the wearer would glide to the ground. Today's parachutes can travel for distances of more than 322 kilometres (200 miles).

11   Use tape on the underside of Hang-Glider 3 to hold down the flaps. Set aside.

12   With an adult's help, measure and cut a piece of skewer the same length as Hang-Glider 4's centre fold. Tape the skewer in place. Set aside.

13   With an adult's help, measure and cut pieces of skewer the same length as Hang-Glider 5's angled edges. Tape the skewers into place.

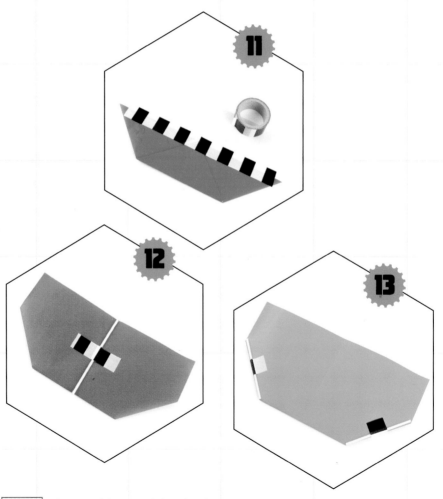

 FACT The world record for the longest hang glide was set in 2012. Dustin Martin and Jonny Durand glided 764 kilometres (474.7 miles). Durand also holds speed records, gliding more than 90 km (56 miles) per hour during a 300 km (186 mile) round trip.

14 To fly, pinch the back of the glider's wing with your index finger and thumb. Release with a gentle, forward push. The higher you hold it to launch, the further it will glide.

15 Practise flying each glider a few times. Then test them. See which glider travels the furthest.

 FACT Taping the wings will reduce aerodynamic drag. The paper clip adds weight to the front of the glider, giving it more stability. The skewers add rigidity to the wing, which allows for better airflow. Which modifications – or combination of modifications – helps the hang-glider travel the furthest?

TRY THIS Test your hang-gliders out on different weather days. Warm, dry air creates rising columns of hot air called thermals. These columns help keep hang-gliders flying. Steady winds help gliders go straight and far.

ZOOMING ZIP LINE

The previous projects focused on gliding or falling gently to the ground. But what if you could use a wheel to glide further and faster? Here's a fun way to move without a road or ramp. Build a zip line from a few simple supplies. Geronimo!

 **YOU'LL NEED**

> masking tape

> 3 metres (3 yards) of string

> wire twist tie

> sewing machine bobbin

> toy figure

STEPS

1. Tape one end of the string to a tabletop or windowsill.

2. Secure the other end of the string to a chair or stool that is lower than the tabletop or windowsill.

3. Thread a wire twist tie through the hole in the bobbin.

4. Place the bobbin on the zip line and use the wire twist tie to attach the toy figure.

34

3 Make cuts in the middle of both rectangles from one edge to the centre.

4 Slide the rectangles together by overlapping the cuts. Hot glue the places where they meet to make a paddle.

5 Squeeze some hot glue into a bead hole. Push the pointy end of a skewer in through the other end. Repeat with the second skewer.

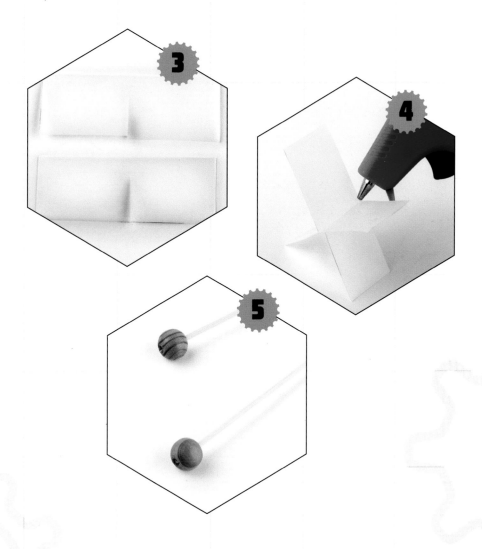

6   Hot glue the skewers to the sides of the bottle.

7   Loop the rubber band over both skewers. Slide half the paddle through the rubber band to hold the paddle in place.

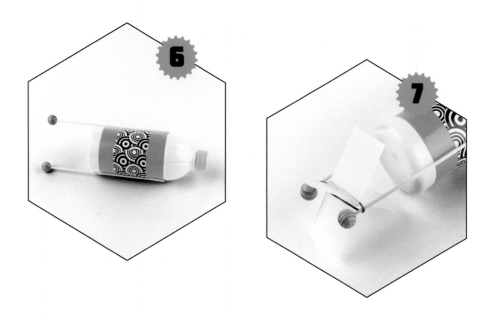

8 Turn the paddle until the rubber band is tightly wound. Put the boat in the water and release it.

 FACT When you place your boat in the water, a force called buoyancy works against the weight of the boat to make it float. Gravity pulls the boat down, and buoyancy pushes the boat up, so it stays on the surface of the water.

TRY THIS Winding the rubber band around the paddle stores elastic potential energy. Once you release the paddle, the rubber band's potential energy is converted to kinetic energy for the paddle. The motion of the paddle pushes against the water and propels the boat across the surface of the water. What happens if you add another rubber band? Does adding many more make a difference?

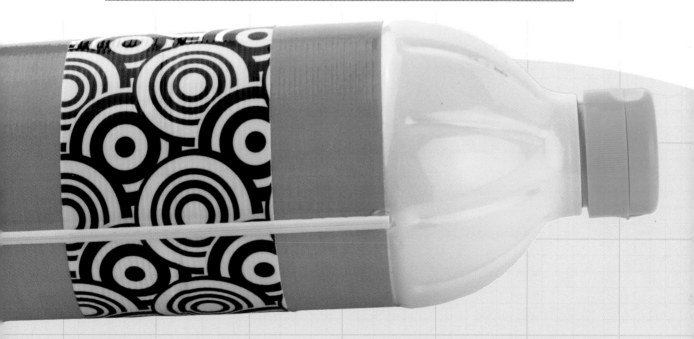

MINI MOTOR PROPELLER CAR

You won't need to rely on wind, ramps or rubber bands with this powerful little car! It moves with the help of a propeller and battery-powered motor. Have fun with electronics by making a simple circuit.

YOU'LL NEED

> plastic food container with lid

> ruler

> two drinking straws

> two skewers

> four plastic wheels

> hot glue and hot glue gun

> utility knife

> mini motor with gear

> propeller

> switch

> electrical tape

> 2 AA battery holder with leads

> 2 AA batteries

> large googly eyes

STEPS

1 Open the container. Measure the width of the container and add 2.5 cm.

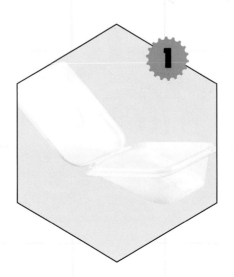

2 Measure and cut two straws and skewers to the measurement you took in step 1.

3 Slide the skewers through the straws. Glue wheels on both ends of the skewers to make axles.

4 Hot glue the straws to the underside of the container.

5 Ask an adult to cut a small rectangle in the centre of the container's lid.

6 Hot glue the motor to the outside of the container lid. It should be centred towards the back.

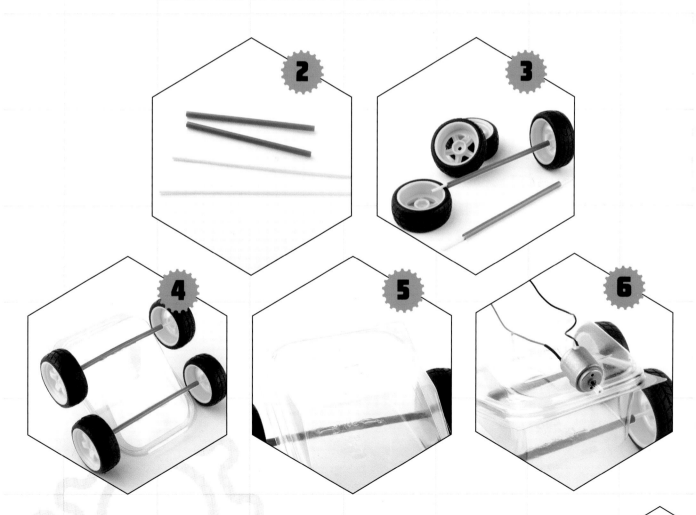

7   Use hot glue to attach the propeller to the motor.

8   Attach the switch to the front of the top with hot glue. Connect the red lead from the motor to the switch with electrical tape.

9   Place the battery holder and batteries inside the plastic container. Use electrical tape to hold them in place. Push the leads through the rectangle in the container's lid, and close the container.

10   Attach the black wire from the battery pack to the remaining terminal on the switch. Secure with tape.

11   Attach the remaining black and red wires. Make sure the switch is in the "off" position.

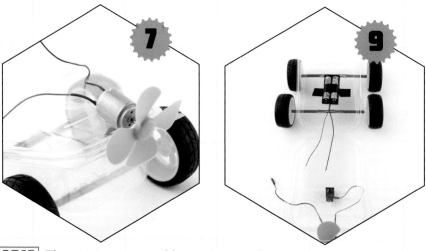

FACT The mini motor and batteries send power to the propeller to make it spin. The force that pushes the vehicle forward is called thrust. The propeller is what creates thrust.

The batteries also store chemical potential energy. By completing the circuit, some of that chemical potential energy becomes electrical energy. The electrical energy is converted to kinetic energy, which powers the propeller.

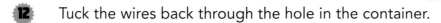

12 Tuck the wires back through the hole in the container.

13 Attach googly eyes with hot glue.

14 When you're ready, flip the switch and watch your car take off!

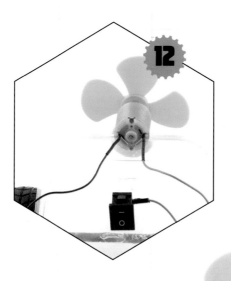

TRY THIS Will your motorised car make it up your Test Track? Play with the track's angles and find out how tough your car really is.

FIND OUT MORE

BOOKS

100 Science Experiments, Georgina Andrews (Usborne, 2012)

101 Great Science Experiments, Neil Ardley (DK Children, 2015)

Experiments with Forces (Read and Experiment), Isabel Thomas (Raintree, 2015)

Forces and Motion (Essential Physical Science), Angela Royston (Raintree, 2014)

WEBSITES

www.bbc.com/bitesize/articles/zxw6gdm
Learn more about water and air resistance.

www.dkfindout.com/uk/science/forces-and-motion
Find out more about forces and motion.